In the Murk of Life

An Anthology of Poetry

Imali J. Abala & Christopher Okemwa
(Editors)

Copyright © 2019 Nsemia Inc. Publishers

All rights reserved

This publication may not be reproduced, in whole or in part, by any means including photocopying or any information storage or retrieval system, without the specific and prior written permission of the author and publisher.

This book is sold subject to the condition that it shall not, by way of trade or otherwise, be re-sold, hired out, or otherwise circulated without the author's or publisher's prior consent in any form of binding or cover other than that in which it is published and without a similar condition including this condition being imposed on the subsequent purchaser.

First Edition: September 2019
Published by Nsemia Inc. Publishers (www.nsemia.com)

Edited By: Imali Abala & Christopher Okemwa
Cover Concept: Imali J. Abala & Christopher Okemwa
Cover Concept Illustration: Robert Maina Kambo
Cover Design: Linda Kiboma
Layout: Bethsheba Nyabuto
Production: Matunda Nyanchama

Note for Librarians:
A cataloguing record for this book is available from Library and Archives Canada.

ISBN: 978-1-926906-83-6

Acknowledgments

Our special thanks go to Carnegie African Diaspora Fellowship Program without which this project would not have come to fruition, and Ohio Dominican University and Kisii University for their indispensable support. Of notable mention are Dr. Theresa Holleran and Dr. Nemwel Aming'a who played a crucial role in the application process, Sarah Elvey, Linet Kombo and Beth Nyamanga.

Preface

In the Murk of Life is one-of-a kind poetry anthology about contemporary life in Kenya. The collection is artistically crafted and addresses the timeless and universal question: what does it mean to be human? The answer to this question varies from poet-to-poet, contextualized by a myriad of experiences in each writer's life. Thus, each piece in the collection is unique, especially in addressing themes of love, disappointment, illness, death and destruction, and corruption and politics. Written in lyrical, free verse, and pantoum styles, each poet's economic use of language paints vivid and evocative images for readers revealing challenges of life in post-colonial Kenya. For example, John Kamau Njoroge's "Torn by Cancer" and Naomi Wanjiku Mwangi's "A Silent Murderer" address the rawness of cancer, man's foe, and its effect in people's lives. While in Biwott Asbel Kiprotich's "I Should," the speaker struggles with a gigantic conundrum: to keep or end a life; the poem has a surprising resolution. And in Dinah Nyokoa Kwalanda's "My Dress, My Choice," a young female speaker empowers herself by claiming her sensual being against the overt sexual discrimination endemic in patriarchic cultures. Thus, readers of *In the Murk of Life* will be enriched both emotionally and spiritually by this collection because it is a well-crafted human story, since human struggle knows no boundaries.

Table of Contents

Acknowledgments iii
Preface v
LEWIS WAMWANDA 1
    I am 1
    Tax Collectors 2
    The Sacrifices We Make 3
IMMACULATE NYAWIRA MUTHONI 5
    Betrayal 5
    It's Him I Want 6
    Between Me and Mine 7
OTILA TITUS ODHIAMBO 8
    The Politics 8
JOHN KAMAU NJOROGE 9
    Torn Apart by Cancer 9
    Sad Little Bird 10
    A Knight in the Night 11
KIPRONO MOSES BETT 12
    I Must Go! 12
BIWOTT ASPEL KIPROP 13
    I Should 13
    Shall Not 15
AUMA MERVINE AUMA 16
    Corruption 16
NAOMI WANJIKU MWANGI 18
    A Silent Murderer 18
    Shame 20

- AURELLIA ATIENO 21
  - Disheartening Society... 21
- KAAN IVINE CHELANGAT 22
  - The Sea Shore 22
- MOSE EUGENE MORANG'A 23
  - Life.. 23
  - The Place We Call Home 24
- MWANZIA MUENI MONICAH 25
  - My Sweet Granny 25
  - The Sea of Sand 26
  - The Twilight Ray 27
- KIPKOSGEI JEPKORIR WINNY.. 28
  - Death Hunger Menace 28
- MWITHIMBU JOY MUKAMI 29
  - In the Midst 29
- DINAH NYAKOA KWALANDA 30
  - My Dress, My Choice.. 30
  - My Love... 31
  - Betrayal 32
- CALVINCE ODHIAMBO.. 34
  - My Twin 34
- FAMBA EVANS ALLAN 36
  - She Shouldn't Do this to Me 36
- KWAMBOKA ANNAH 37
  - He Was no More 37
  - The Massacre 38
- MBYATI MERCY MUTANO 39
  - The Map.. 39
- MUBISI JEDIDA NDUBI.. 40
  - Hurt... 40

OUSA BRILLIAN JUNE	41
Asset of the City	41
VALERIA JEPCHUMBA	42
A Skilled Leadership	42
EVANS MWENDWA MUTIE	43
You!	43
NEKESA ZIPPORAH	45
Cursed Generation	45
My Soul	47
CLIFF OYUGI KERAGE	48
Voyage	48
Drip Drop	50
Demons	51
ELLY OMULLO	53
Will Do It Tomorrow	53
IMALI J. ABALA	55
I am	55
Restless Soul	57
My Long Road to the Ballot	58
HARRISON OMAMBIA ANYANGO	59
Holy Grail	59
CHRISTOPHER OKEMWA	60
Don't Cry	60
About the Editors	63

LEWIS WAMWANDA

I am

I Write what I am
My art can fill the heart
Like quenching thirst
In a dry hot desert

I am, what I write
For my pens are my thoughts
My words are my soul
Inking them into lines

I am a writer, a poet
Lines that flow
Trickling on a steep cliff
Seeps through the vein

I am a poem
With letters and words
Bringing the death to life
Shaping the words to lines

Tax Collectors

Ding dong, goes the bell
The door opens wide
They Rush in and out
Like busy bees on errands

They flood the gates
With big round bellies
Like huge ripe pumpkins
Collecting notes and cents

They stink of filth
Flies for followers
Buzzing hymns of hunger
To devour the cents collected

Tax collectors,
Collecting taxes from husbands
And sometimes leave "change"
Which sprout after nine months

Ding Dong, goes the bell
They flood in the open bars
Carrying empty hungry bellies
Later filled with taxed booze

The Sacrifices We Make

You will feed us with honey and milk
To bribe us away from the pain
But the memories will be buried deep within us
Plunging deep down the thoughts of sorrow
Like a small ship lost in the middle of a raging sea
Or a plane in the middle of a stormy night
And silently, within the verge of our sorrow
We will summon death for comfort
And take pain with us
To ease the burden in our hearts

We will laugh together 'till midnight
To give you hopes of triumph
And a sense of victory and pride
But when we lay silently in our beds
In the cold lonely nights
The buried memories will find their way out
To torment and lure us to pain
Mocking and making fun at us
As we bath in tears of our sorrows
And fighting ourselves back to slumber

Nights will not be time to sleep
For fear will be roaming at the darkest hours
Waiting to pounce on our beaten souls
And take control of the long nights
We will be enslaved by our memories

Tortured by the past bitter pains
To the point of breaking our souls
And killing the little joy we possessed
Extinguishing the light lit years ago
And hope and happiness will float in the dark

We will laugh and smile all day
And you will praise us for our happiness
And urge others to be like us
To follow the steps we ought to make
But you won't understand our griefs
And not notice the masks we wear
That fades as dusk approaches
Leaving us naked, afraid and lonely
And the chains of fear will be put on us
As we wait for our long night of torture

IMMACULATE NYAWIRA MUTHONI

Betrayal

A broken rose
Amidst the depth of shattered trust
Like a mannequin you pose
Overwhelmed with burning lust

Colourful package rotting soul
Diving deep in guile
Just like bad omen -- the presence of an owl
Your lips taste as bitter as bile

The grotesque images flood my mind
Caught pants down, tongue tied
In your bed of lies you were bound
Biting the forbidden fruits, tightly held

How could you break such a fragile heart?
Unveil the darkest part of my soul,
The knife of betrayal pierced more
than cupid's arrow
In dismay I am bound
But your infidelity makes me writhe in pain,
Your love, cold like rain
Has caused me to depart

It's Him I Want

I must have left my dignity at the door
Writhing, gnashing in the pain I bore
If I could only rewrite the stars
Maybe raise the bar

You be my caffeine and English muffin
Each morning
Getting lost in your eyes, mourning
Our heart a faucet scarlet love pouring
Give me the antidote – in it I be drowning

But you are just a dream, waking up is a nightmare
A man as sweet as you is rare
Dear owner, give me the remedies
I get rid of this malady
I sing with him in melody
I don't want a parody
It's him I want.

Between Me and Mine

Between me and mine
Shivers down my spine
Sweating, breathing vehemently
Hearts racing
Intense breathing
Beings mating

Cupid's arrow pierced too deep
A gem I will keep
Love pouring like a faucet,
Like Romeo and Juliet on set

Cracked ground has been watered
Void spaces neatly packed
Mend the heart that was tattered
Healed that which once ached

Between me and mine
New is always divine
Does away with the bitter
And am changed for the better

OTILA TITUS ODHIAMBO

The Politics

Politicians are not like what we feel,
Apart from who we are executing dodge of kill
Agony of severance is there; will it heal?

Many are playing backroom for our Nation's wheel
But Homo sapiens are on both side of the hill,
Politicians are not like what we feel!

Make good decisions minus any deal,
Avoid listening to those who are psychologically ill,
Agony of severance is there; will it heal?

No need for war; let's fight for food,
To fathom ourselves we need to apply skills,
Politicians are not like what we feel!

Happy for hosting flags, a kid's zeal,
Let them live their own anxiety and will,
Agony of severance is there; will it heal?

Fame of humanness no one can steal,
Difference between borders who will fill,
Politicians are not like what we feel.
Agony of severance is there; will it heal?

JOHN KAMAU NJOROGE

Torn Apart by Cancer

He raised his limp withered hand
To touch the big lump on his throat
It seemed to grow bigger day-by-day
And more painful one second away.

He touched the big lump on his throat
And gazed sadly into the dark oblivion
'Cause it grew more painful by the second
Oozing thick stinky pus all the while.

He gazed sadly into the dark oblivion
And pressed the big lump on his throat
It oozed thick stinking pus all the while
His throat felt as though choked with bile.

He pressed the big lump on his throat
And twice a smile he tried to feign
But his throat felt as though choked with bile
So he lay on his side in untold pain.

Twice a smile he tried to feign
But the lump seemed to grow bigger day-by-day
He lay on his side in untold pain
And in surrender raised his limp withered hand.

Sad Little Bird

I've heard this little bird sing
Sad melodies that in my ears ring
And drive my soul awake
To console this little bird by the lake
That sing sad melodies of her own
To lament why it is dawn.

I've seen this little bird
Follow the scent of flowers that bud
And painfully suck
As if causing her luck
And reluctantly fly away
To her nest where she lay.

I've seen this little bird
Isolating her lonely self
And burying her poor body
Deep in thick bushes
To escape the approach of fellow birds.

I've watched this little bird
Fly swiftly when darkness approaches
Singing sweet melodies of merry
That someday darkness will reign
On her life full of sorrow
And die a painless death.

A Knight in the Night

When darkness engulfs the world at night
And the moon gleams in darkness as stars twinkle in jest
He creeps out of his hiding place, for beauty has caught his sight.

Big of body and great of might
He steals into the night, his footsteps echoing in the forest
When darkness engulfs the world at night.

He keeps hidden from the moonlight
And when he sees fierce warriors in their rest
He creeps out of his hiding place, for beauty has caught his sight.

His heart throbs yearning for a fight
Because only then can he emerge as the best
When darkness engulfs the world at night.

Killing the warriors, he creeps into hiding thinking it right
To spare all women to drain his lust.
He creeps out of his hiding place, for beauty has caught his sight.

Deep in thought, he watches a bird in flight
As he kills his victims quite fast
And darkness engulfs the world at night
As he creeps out of his hiding place, for beauty has caught his sight.

KIPRONO MOSES BETT

I Must Go!

Farewell my friends, for I must go!
I have been called to fight
My country needs me that I know
To aid it in its plight.

I have been called to fight
It is my solemn duty bound
To aid the country in its plight
I haste as trumpets sound.

I cannot surely now delay
My farewells have been said
To haste as trumpets sound; I'm away
With swift and eager tread.

Come death, defeat of glory
My country needs me that I know
And though I'll miss you surely
Farewell my friends, for I must go!

BIWOTT ASPEL KIPROP

I Should

A sight so touching, in its majesty
Beauty of the morning, so silent;
Cold hearted it was
Dumping *it* at ease was easy

Everything looked precious except *it*
Further around the world, I could travel with *it*
Getting a good place to dump *it*,
Honouring *it*, giving a last bow: Goodbye

In daylight's bright presence,
Judging *it* first would change my thought
Keenly avoiding the good side of my mind
Looking uneasy like an old drunk witch
Moving with stagger to the door and switch

New life will begin after dumping *it*
Opening a new door to my life, maybe of troubles
Praying it be good, not laced with sorrow
Questions of my interrogative mind avoided
Resting the case of what if the unexpected happens?

In the Murk of Life

Should I attempt?
To move ahead and put *it* under the ground?
Under the hiding ground?
Various thoughts run on my mind like a tsunami.

Well, I should do, came the decision of mind
Xian nature of me came across like the wind
You'll face consequences of your chosen call;
Zero actions crossed my mind!

Shall Not

I chose her because she was the best
I didn't care about the rest
I do rate her as the best

She would relax like a bird in the nest
As I looked at her chest
I chose her because she was the best

Much has been said about her
That she is among the evil girls
Still, I do rate her as the best

I am here to love her,
Not listen to what they say
I chose her because she is the best

I loved her because she was different
Convinced that none is better than her
Still I do rate her as the best

I still love her and believe she is too
Beautiful, caring and with etiquette too!
Despite advices against her,
I chose her because she was the best

AUMA MERVINE AUMA

Corruption

Again, how can I stand strong?
But this game has become a song.
Corruption, a game?
Damn shame!
Every day they take an oath
Far as even from North to South
Grabbing and bleeding our country to death.

Hey! Bribes itch my country men
Ian and others touch their mane
Just whistling, with hands in their pockets
Kind of moving like rockets
Lazily as they wait in queue
Mmh! It is performed like a cue
Now others wait in vain.

Oops! Corruption stinks
Poorly, our skins it stings
Quickly numbering is to hail
Rapidly our country sinking to hell
So, through the gates of impurity
The forgotten is purity
Unfortunately, every man for himself.

Very true the fire is fierce
Whole day ready to pierce
Xians, the souls that resist
Yearly they refuse to assist
Zeal of corruption is the master.

NAOMI WANJIKU MWANGI
A Silent Murderer

After writhing and wriggling
Before our puzzled faces
Calling out our names
Demanding this and that, your
Ears didn't hear my calling

Forgive me Mama; I never saw it coming!
Gone are the days I saw your crescent smile
Having been perfectly placed upon your face
Indeed, by our creator. I remember the
Joyful moments we shared, but this
Killer of souls suddenly snatched it from us
Leaving us desperate and dejected.

Mama, I wish I possessed the knowledge
Now; you couldn't be suffering from this
Ogre-monster, a silent murderer!
Perhaps, if I had cash, I would have
Quickly taken you abroad where
Real cures are and happen, but
Somehow, someday, at some moment,
This will come to an end!

Unfortunately Mama, it is in
Vain; can't fight this devil-cancer. It
Walks with so many soldiers. Mama, doctors'
X-ray will succeed, revealing your healed body
You will come back to us again. Mama, your
Zero hour is not yet her!

Shame

That very time I missed it
And the nausea got to me
It dawned on me: I got it,
But damn, I couldn't sustain it
I had to get rid of it!

Or should I let it live?
But why?
Will I withstand the mockery?
Or the burning razor-sharp words
From friends and neighbors?

But why should I deny you life?
Why should I?
Is it your fault you were conceived?
Is it?
I'll let you live sweetheart.

Like a bird, I will feed you
Like a bee, I will protect you
Like an angel, I will watch over you.
I will love you to infinity
I will let you live my child.

AURELLIA ATIENO

Disheartening Society

Hungry and helpless they were
Begging bare-footed at the streets
What a disheartening society?

Tired and almost knocked by their cars
They had no one to lend them a hand
Hungry and helpless they were.

Where did the kind-hearted people go?
Those who could help the helpless, oh!
What a disheartening society?

Mercedes and Landcruisers passed over and over
Mother and child as thin as a starved cat
Hungry and helpless they were.

Does it cost much to lend a hand?
Does it ache much to empathize?
Hungry and helpless they were,
What a disheartening society?

KAAN IVINE CHELANGAT

The Sea Shore

An amazing sight
Beautiful to behold
Crystals of sand all around, I sat
Dabbing in the water and
Enjoying the cool breeze
Facing the Eastern side
Giraffes tall and splendid
Hovering over the mangroves
Indifferent of anything
Just an awesome sight
Keenly I stood
Leaning on a palm tree
Miles away to the horizon
Nothing but masses and masses
Of many waters
Pacing from end to end
Quickly and pacific
Racing while singing
Silently to the tunes of the sea
Unveiling the large
Vacantness
Waddling on the beaches
Xanthochroic kids
Yelling and calling
Zealously to the sea

MOSE EUGENE MORANG'A

Life

Reality dawns on everyone
That they don't care
With no houses, people are left

Corruption is the order of the day
Even for a job, you have to pay
Reality dawns on everyone

Food and fuel prices have risen
Hunger bites the citizen, demolitions rock shanties
With no houses, people are left

Life is hard in the ghetto
Muggings and murder on the rise
Reality dawns on everyone

With no power or unity
Citizens are left suffering
Hope is all they haven't lost

No one dares to talk
For fear of being lynched or arrested
Reality dawns on everyone
That they're alone, not government

The Place We Call Home

A Ray of hope
Builds up, expectations rise
Cries and wails die down
Distant memories, must all chaos remain
Elevated to presidency, he throws a party
Forgetting those who voted, us
Gives jobs and tenders to family
Hovering above us, police helicopters
Ironically, my mother is robbed, murdered
Joyful they are, always
Killings they cause, don't face them
Luckily or unlucky, they'll come for votes
Money, once again will buy them votes
Never will we learn, to say no
Or at least choose someone better
Pointless are, their talks at rallies, as we
Queue for a fifty shilling note
Raising our voices
Shouting praises for "His Excellency" and CO
Time's up, they leave, satisfaction on their faces
Under the dull moon we sleep
Viciously, hunger bites
While they sit at the buffet
X convicts for corruption and fraud
Yet undauntedly, they still embezzle funds
Zippers to the neck, sleep takes over.

MWANZIA MUENI MONICAH

My Sweet Granny

Her bending back,
Her feet wobbled,
Age had beaten her up,
Tired she was like a pilgrim.

Her feet wobbled,
Her words though still made sense,
Tired she was like a pilgrim,
Her advice still rang in my wits.

Her words though still made sense,
Her zeal and will made it more real,
Her advice still rang in my wits,
A stage had come.

Her zeal and will made it more real,
They call it old age,
A stage had come,
I admire her golden age.

They call it old age,
Age had beaten her up,
I admire her golden age,
Her bending back.

In the Murk of Life

The Sea of Sand

This fateful sea sand is where I want to stay to the end,
It is the sand dunes that we fell and rolled on and on,
It is where our eyes met, I will kiss you to the end.

It is the storm that made her hold me tight,
It is the sand dunes, that we fell on and on,
This fateful sea of sand, is where I want to stay to the end

It is the storm that made her hold me tight,
It is the sand dunes we fell on and rolled on and on,
It is where our eyes closed, I will kiss you to the end.

It is in this sea of sand,
That my love was found,
This fateful sea of sand, is where I want to stay to the end.

It is the storm that made her hold me tight,
That my love was found,
It is where our eyes closed, I will kiss you to the end.

It is this sea of sand,
That my love was found,
This fateful sea of sand, is where I want to stay to the end,
It is where our eyes closed, I will kiss you to end.

The Twilight Ray

Oh dear colossal partner
How soon you had me, not soil
Washed all the muck on my back
Got hold of me tightly
And the grip's tighter than my jeans?

You are a rare morning ray
Desired by all that breathes
Everybody steals a glance as you pass
Gasps at your elegance as you go
And wishes you could stay, a moment

I recently lost my seat
In the peers parliament
By promoting a bill to the members
To avoid stealing glances at you
And I am still here, with intuitions

Come to me, peak of my life
Hold my desperate hand
Take away every love in me
Even the one for white t-shirts
And let my kids call you, "Dad"

KIPKOSGEI JEPKORIR WINNY

Death Hunger Menace

The summer ended
The holidays ended
New Year is welcomed
The sun rises; the sun sets
No rains forecasted

The Western and Eastern places
The North and Southern places
The Central regions and coasts
No rains forecasted, lands are dry
Diseases and pests migrate
Plants die, cows die, people die
Society cries crocodile tears

The leaders quarrel over non-important issues
No relief, no food; birds die
The country perishes while people cry of hunger
Leaders only protect our country's name
Black and red cars in the city seen

Men with big stomachs laugh
Ooh God, come and save Israel
Our nation needs you like Israelites
Please change the minds of our leaders
When can our country change?
Hunger, hunger move away from us

MWITHIMBU JOY MUKAMI

In the Midst

Left, Right, Centre
Am in between
Posing with my mask
Like that liquid in the flask

Call it bitter-sweet sorrow
Or nostalgic Joy
Like those clouds
Up there in the sky
Am in the midst

For we all have those days
Like the blaze
Then after the cool
Or in the mid
Knowing deep down when dawn
Arrives
Sometimes we are in the midst.

DINAH NYAKOA KWALANDA
My Dress, My Choice

I put on a short skirt,
They say it's too short and tight,
That my thighs are too large for it,
I never asked for their opinion,
My dress, my choice!

They say it's too short and tight,
As they keep throwing glances at it,
That a longer skirt would be right,
I never asked for their opinion,
My dress, my choice.

As they keep throwing glances at it,
They are hit by a fast moving motorist,
I am scolded for causing the accident,
I never asked for their opinion,
My dress, my choice.

They are hit by a fast moving motorist,
When all they needed was to mind their sight,
And mind their business a little bit,
I never asked for their opinion,
My dress, my choice.

My Love

Telling him I love him is not just enough,
Every time I look at him,
I smile as adrenaline rushes through my body.

As if it's not enough, I become breathless,
Helplessly touching his beards,
Telling him I love him is not just enough.

His scent so sweet, I cannot let go of him,
Hugging me so tightly, cuddling me with love,
I smile as adrenaline rushes through my body.

His kisses so fine, ever lingering on my lips,
Yearning for more, every time he comes to sight,
Telling him I love him is not just enough.

He carries me in his arms, like a baby I fold myself,
Hanging my legs in the air, trusting him not to fall,
I begin to smile and adrenaline rushes through my body.

All I pray for is to marry him,
For he is the only man of my dreams,
Every time I think of my future, he appears,
Telling him I love him is not just enough.

Betrayal

Am not you,
But you keep on complaining about my personality,
Can't you just mend your personality first?
Don't judge me, you know nothing about me.

Enrolling me to your crew was a good idea,
Fortunately, I found a rare company,
Gladly following you around,
Honestly telling you my mind.

I never thought of your betrayal,
Just an innocent soul I was,
Knowing you will be the secret keeper,
Little did I know you were a traitor.

My heart lied to me,
Not once but many times,
On the very day I trusted you,
Put all my hopes in you.

Quite excited about you,
Resting my worries on you,
Should have thought of the consequences,
Trusting you was the worst mistake.

Unfortunately, I cannot reverse it,
Vowing never to repeat the same,
Whole heartedly I forgive you,
Xylophone will be my new company,
Yes I will play it and sing,
Zipping my mouth for the better

CALVINCE ODHIAMBO

My Twin

Do take my healthy pen,
Tell you about my lovely twin,
Smells like a garden rose at dawn,
One fresh from a newly opened bud.

I call her twin,
'Cause she's one amongst ten,
And I wonder how and when,
He modelled here there in heaven,
So might be the reason,
Why she's the only one,
Whose head I see high enough,
To communicate to the heavens,
My lovely twin prays for me to God.

Her head up close to God, and her legs,
Her legs down on the earth,
She's for me, the earth,
She's for him, the heavens.

Makes me worry less when near,
I don't have to go for the mirror,
Even when at the rear,
'Cause my twin is informed in prior,
And does all her duties with no failure.

Corrects me when am on the wrong,
Teaches me all night long,
And at bed she stays so strong,
Until we make love a song,
Which only the two of us understand.

FAMBA EVANS ALLAN

She Shouldn't Do this to Me

I hate writing poetry,
If only my teacher knew,
She shouldn't do this to me.

It's even worse than geometry,
It's terrible thing to do,
I hate writing poetry!

It's very plain to see,
I tell you it's true,
She shouldn't do this to me.

This is my final plea,
I can't write this for you,
I hate writing poetry!

I can't write a poem like Persephone,
That would be hard to do,
She shouldn't do this to me.

I'd rather watch TV,
Or try something new,
I hate writing poetry,
She shouldn't do this to me.

KWAMBOKA ANNAH

He Was no More

In the terrifying morning,
As the birds chirped,
And the trees danced,
The cold wind blew.

A painful cry I heard,
It was from the front yard,
Quickly I ran for aid,
Oooh, mama, what is happening?

He was no more,
His breath was long gone,
To the spirits world, Papa had gone,
Out of a mere sickness.

Very cold were his feet,
And his hands, as white as chalk,
Still with his humble face laid there,
Not moving, eyes closed.

They carried him away,
Sorrowfully, I mourned and mourned,
Hoping he could come back to life,
But no, he had gone, gone forever.

The Massacre

Aloud, I shouted terrified,
Begging and begging for mercy,
Crying with tears rolling down,
Danger had befallen us!
Every street was startled,
From west to east entangled,
Grounds were not ours,
Houses were burnt to a mess,
Indeed, no hope was left to behold,
Jointly, we were pushed on,
Keenly tied and lead like sheep,
Lamenting oooh without shield,
Male folks of our land,
Oriented to save us,
Piercing, pricking, the enemy,
Questing to revive our army,
Ruined from toil and struggle,
Soaked in a bloody sweat were humbled,
Their effort hopelessly ended,
Under own leaders, humbled,
Venomed with pain and hatred,
We became villains in our own land,
Yawning every day for restoration and,
Zero became our position, till now.

MBYATI MERCY MUTANO

The Map

Tap!!Tap!! Tap!! Tap!!
Drops of water fall bit-by-bit,
On the once beautiful map.

Destroying and beaten by age,
The water drops take turns on it,
Tap!! Tap!! Tap!! Tap!!.

The map that describes our landscape,
That showed our beautiful country,
Oh!! The once beautiful map.

Now torn and wretched,
But the drops have no mercy,
Tap!! Tap!! Tap!! Tap!!

Undergoing the pain bit-by-bit,
Writhing, but with no one to help,
Tap!!Tap!!Tap!!Tap!!
On the once beautiful map.

MUBISI JEDIDA NDUBI

Hurt

At the corridors she stands,
Seething in pain and despair,
Owning a broken soul,
A heart full of wounds.

Seething in pain and despair,
She reminisces the past,
He'd won her trust,
And turned out a monster.

Reminiscing the past,
The order of the events crossing her mind,
The moon the only witness,
Of the untold wretchedness.

The order of the events crossing her mind,
Pinned to the wall like Jesus on the cross,
His pestle pounding her pride,
His smile marking her wickedness

On the wall like Jesus on the cross,
Possessing a broken soul,
His smile marking his wickedness,
Her heart full of wounds.

OUSA BRILLIAN JUNE

Asset of the City

Wherever she did a shimmy,
With her over enticing bottom,
Basking in the vanity of being desired,
In the periodic flash lights,
You made me curse my mind,
For the refreshment,
Of the nostalgia musty nights,
Days back then in the pub's darkness.

Her ever tantalizing beauty,
Her captivating smiles and
More than just a normal,
V-like attractive and mouth-watering,
Awesome cleavage,
Made me curse my birthday,
For I was soon dissipating my youth.

I longed for her features,
Revealing –not- lying trifles,
Pegged to her curves so intimately,
Caused her sharp nipples visible,
And my eyes were imprisoned,
At the sight of the city goodness!!

VALERIA JEPCHUMBA

A Skilled Leadership

A three-legged stool'
Beneath that *mugumo* tree,
Comfortably sat the leader,
Driving his leadership emotions,
Expecting good views and feedback,
From his loyal people,
Guarantee of his courtesy,
Having held the leadership mantle,
In accordance to the law,
Judging justly their mistakes,
Keeping the promises he made,
Leading the way to stay,
Moving swiftly like blowing wind,
Not in pretense to bring harm,
Opting for the best from them,
Performing designed duties perfectly,
Quarrelling with no person,
Rendering him being perfect,
So it was him to be,
Temporarily and later permanently,
Uniting his country people,
Vowing to do till eternity,
Whispering the joys of his heart,
Xylem, phloem I will co-operate as so,'
Yielding good citizens forever,
Zeal his leadership morale.

EVANS MWENDWA MUTIE
You!

Arise and shine dear. They have come for you,
Bake them the best cake. They wait to taste you,
Clean yourself and wear fragrance. They want to see you,
Dance for them dear. Let your waist praise you,
Eat with them dear. They want to sit with you,
Fill them with desire and lust. Let them want you.

Give them hope dear. Make them not leave you,
Hold them by the arms. Let them feel you,
Insight their yearnings dear. Let them hunger for you,
Just tease them. Let them smile with you,
Kindly treat them dear. They are here just for you,
Leave them talking about you. Make them speak nice of you,

Meet their needs dear. They will like you,
Never fall for them dear. They might trick you,
Open your heart cautiously. Be choosy on wins over you,
Please dear. We don't have to lose you,
Quiet sister. Don't cry of these words that I say to you,
Reach not out for these easy fruits. They are sour, they'll hurt you.

In the Murk of Life

Stay with Mum dear. Don't let your youth deceive you,
Trust our family sister. We will never fail you,
Use your intellect dear. Beauty and brains should prevail in you,
Vet them well dear. Suitors will be there for you,
We wish you well sister. May the Almighty be with you,

Exophthalmia they will suffer. Just ogling at you,
You are smarter than them dear. Let them not control you,
Zest won't give you the best suitor. Patience will do for you.

NEKESA ZIPPORAH

Cursed Generation

Astonished and sunk in the ocean of thought,
By the tender behavior of the youths,
Controlled by the shabbiness of their bodies,
Digging into the flower as busy as a bee,
Emphatic enough to test the sweetness of the nectar,
Fit and muscular, being driven by the lust of their flesh.

Gay and lesbianism being part of their lifestyle,
Headed by the insight of their peers,
Interested on the bloody lips and bleached faces,
Just thinking inside the box,
Kissing and cuddling carelessly,
Little did they know, there is a dreaded disease.

Mounting on every woman like a cow on heat,
Naughty they are!! Their mind is a devils workshop,
Obedience and patience is no more,
Perpetuated by their evil thoughts in the new generation,
Quite busy killing their future,
Risking life and burying themselves alive. Ooh no!!

In the Murk of Life

Today we have resolved, not to defile ourselves,
Undefeated we are!!,
Vows that are immature must be broken,
War has been declared and machete are sharpened,
Xylophones are bitten to create awareness,
Young people,
WE MUST FIGHT with the
Zeal of reforming and transforming the new life.

My Soul

Come here my soul, near the sea,
Hasten here my passion as you can see,
To discover my hidden passion without a fee,
My passion which is ever hidden under a tree.

Hasten here my passion as you can see,
Calling upon you my soul, do not complain,
My passion which is ever hidden under a tree,
As you leave my mind in turmoil forever.

Calling upon you my soul, do not complain,
So that you can make my dreams find a way,
As you leave my mind in turmoil forever,
And refusing to discover the hidden passion ever.

So that you can make my dreams find away,
And stop it from swaying back and forth,
And refusing to discovering my hidden passion ever,
That comes closer my soul, so that to pave a way.

And stop it from swaying back and forth,
Calling upon my soul, do not complain,
My clock will burst out of the skin,
Come here my soul, near the sea.

CLIFF OYUGI KERAGE

Voyage

Like a solitary wayfarer on voyage,
I have travelled across briary mountains of pain
Roved through deserted swamps of dejection
Sailed against the tides in stormy seas of sorrow
Swirled by emotional whirlwind in the isle of fate
And lost myself in a gloomy forest of forlornness

I have seen mornings blossom like roses
And evenings wither like autumn leaves
The sun sublime beyond the skyline
And dark days reign the aura

I have heard a cacophony of cricket chirrups ring in my mind
Suicide demons fighting in my brain
The moon peeking at me like a spy
And the stars beaming faintly from the sky
I have lost myself into a series of emotional detention
And seen my dreams of better days turn into nightmares

I have seen dark clouds form in my eyelids like black wool
And heavy rains fall down my cheeks
I have felt my world torn apart
Draining my future hopes and aspirations
And the heavens giving me a taunting stare

My key to success has drowned in a pool of tears
The world around me has scorned me like an alien
I have borne the heavy weight of my swollen heart
Swallowed the bitter herb of truth
And tasted the sweetness of betrayal
Each time my shadow walks out of me
And leaves me dumped in the ruins
I have been buried each moment a piece of me dies deep within

I have searched through my soul
Looked deep into my past memories
I have found my childhood self-hiding deep within
He has been leading my heart into wounds
Yet still he cries for attention like little baby

I have woken to reality that life is a flowing river full of crocodiles
And I am a wildebeest waiting anxiously at the verge
To cross to the other side where pastures are greener
Where a new dawn is gazing at me with a warm grimace
And the birds are singing with mellifluous melodies
I yearn to walk through the narrow path of bliss over there
And sail through the calm seas of peace and joy.

Drip Drop

Am seated solitary by the window as I watch
The sun go down fading like fog
Grey sheep walks tardily in the sky
Drip drop drop drip drizzling mizzle
Trees dancing to the swishing whistle
Cricket chirps, bird chirrups twitter in the air
Drip drop drop drip drizzling mizzle
Ding-dong ding-dong rings the door
Rub-a-dub rub-a-dub goes my chest
I peep through a hole on my doorknob
The moon peeks at me like a secret agent
Drip drop, drip drop drizzling mizzle
Midnight goes dead silent and fireflies flicker
Squeaks and shrieks fill the ambiance as darkness withers.

Demons

They are back
These demons that torment and devour
I can feel them
Turning an abyss out of the serene place I knew
The aura gone malodorous of their dirty breath
I can feel them burn me up like Mercury
I want to scream the devils out my being
Pull off my hair bit by bit
So to give an outlet to the outside
I am dying inside piece by piece
Feeling as if I am in hell
And burning up in Sulphur
With the hellfire too intense
My spirits pierce through my skin
And the walls of my heart ready to collapse
My own saliva turned up like a concoction
Wearing out my gut into a bitter chime
But what is better?
Is it living up to this suffering?
Or rather should I wave bye to this ideal?

Ouch!!
It cuts through my soul like a burned up dagger
The arrow pointed direct to my fragile heart
The venom is paralyzing me
I want to give up
Put down the ruffle

And let go this struggle
I won't fight a losing battle
I am too weak to survive
Maybe I need a bottle of whiskey
A little intoxicant and some pills
To rescue me from this web
A razor to cut the hell out of these shackles of demons
A tight rope round my neck will ease the pain
I just want to walk out of me
Run fast past these prison of demons
Hide myself in a gloomy forest
Where I will be invisible to my raging devils
I yearn to dwell in the dark land of solitude
Where pain doesn't exist and my emotions will not explode.

ELLY OMULLO

Will Do It Tomorrow

Will do it tomorrow,
For now a piffling slumber,
Trivial slumber,
Won't close m' eyes,
Won't dream.
For my body is hefty,
I mean toxic,
With venom of heavy eyes,
Am dopey,
-really fatigued,
Will do it tomorrow,
That I avow solemnly,
There is much time,
I swallowed some sleeping pills,
Analgesics as you call them,
But see they are sleeping too,
Snoring, catnapping inside me,
Will do it tomorrow,
Am an old young man.
Let me slumber, a modicum of siesta
Want the same dream
I had yesterday,
Was in my own world,
On the royal throne there I was,
Carbonated in princess paraphernalia.

In the Murk of Life

With guards standing beside me,
For accountability of my hair,
In a bungalow I was,
M' parking yard was full,
With elegant, Junoesque, dainty cars.
Whose cost still cost me to know.
So let me slumber, a morsel of drowse.
Will do it tomorrow.

IMALI J. ABALA

I am

I am who I am.
If you care to look,
You'll find me!

You might change my name,
Or clip my tongue,
Or give me your religion,

I am who I am.
Your erasure of me
Need not be my reality!

You might refuse to see me,
Or admit my being,
I am who I am,

Vibrant, vivacious, alive!
I am every inch of myself,
Flesh of my flesh, human!

So, don't tell me you can't see me,
My invisibility is my visibility.
I know myself; seeing, but not seen.

In the Murk of Life

If only you removed
That fog off your eyes,
You'll see me, every atom of my being:

I am who I am!

Restless Soul

O Death, you most feared of man's foe
Come quickly carrying your cup of woe
Lure me into extinction from my rugs of woe
Of my ravaged body, weapon of my destruction;
Goad not my unsuspecting adversaries!
Here I am, take me into your peaceful wings!
Hop not aimlessly over Mung'oma boulders,
Worn in torrential rain, where peripherally you lurk,
Awaiting the innocent unaware for your tender embrace
Here I am, take me into your wings of peace,
Engulf me, itch-by-itch until am no more!
No need hopping from house-to-house,
Already fallen prey to your suffocating darkness,
Unstained with blood a door to bar your entrance,
Not knowing it is you for whom I long and desire.
It is you for whom my heart's bell tolls unabashed.
It is not the end I fear, but the wrath of the living.
Who'll languish in their sorrow in my cessation?
Take me to heaven's glory where I belong.

My Long Road to the Ballot

Yesterday, I stood in queue—
>Ready to cast my vote,
>Hoping against hope
>That change was inevitable.

Yesterday, as I stood in queue—
>The ogre sun baked my darkened skin.
>I tried to bolt the window of my mind
>With the illusion of change, real change,
>As the bitterness of defeat razor-blade my heart.
>Surely, change was my coveted outcome!

Yesterday, I stood in queue—
>I neither saw hope nor glory in my ballot
>As it fell into the cracks of gummy-tainted fingers.
>So my hopes dwindled to the gloom of dusk,
>A painful reminder of the façade of the ballot,
>An outcome long concluded before its inception.

Today, I no longer stand in queue—
>For my heart is still lacerated with the sorrow,
>Raped off any hope for change, yet again;
>Much like the hood-shaped helmet of monkshood
>Raped without mercy by an ugly butterfly's stabbing.
>Yet, I am left to wonder:
>*"What did we do to warrant our defeat?"*

HARRISON OMAMBIA ANYANGO
Holy Grail

Her love was like a resplendent
Holy grail
That any exposure could
Unite a flock of devouts
Like a responsive students
over a gong sound
this could take you quite aback

I'm not quick to wield
upon them, I felt their rapture
Nor careless in abuse
But I still like them less for show
And rather more for use.

CHRISTOPHER OKEMWA

Don't Cry

If I die, don't cry
Because I would become a rose flower
Grow in your flower garden
And exude fragrance
You will pick me during Christmas
Display me during birthdays
Smell me during weddings
I will be part of you
So, if I die, don't cry

If I die, don't be grieved
Because I would become a bumpkin leaf
Grow in your vegetable garden
Pick me for supper in the evenings
Cook me in the kitchen at nights
I will be at the dining table with you
So, if I die, don't be grieved

If I die, don't moan
Because I will become rain
Fall down from the sky
Gather me by the gutters
And wash kitchen utensils with me
I will be in your kitchen
So, if I die, don't moan

If I die, don't scream
Because I will become a tree
Grow in the corner of our homestead
Cut me occasionally for firewood
Keep a heap of me in your kitchen
Make fire and cook *ugali* with me
I will be part of the household
So, if I die, don't scream

Ugali is a Kenyan dough made from maize flour.

About the Editors

Imali J. Abala is a professor of English at Ohio Dominican University (USA) where she teaches literature, creative writing, and college writing courses. She is a published author of many books: The Dreamer, Haughty Boys of Ngoroke, Moody Mood and Red Round Ball, Drum Bits of Terror, A Fallen Citadel (a collection of poetry), The Dilemma of Jahenda: The Teenage Mother, and The Disinherited and Move on, Trufosa. Some of her other works (poetry and short stories) have also appeared in several anthologies in the USA and Uganda.

Christopher Okemwa is a lecturer of literature as well as a director of the School of Post Graduate Studies at Kisii University. He is the founder and director of Kistretch International Poetry Festival in Kenya. His published works range from poetry collections, oral literature, and a short story collection. This is in addition to three children's books and five folktales of the Abagusii, among others. Okemwa's novella *Sabina and the Mystery of the Ogre* won 2015 *Burt Award for African Literature (Kenya)*.

www.ingramcontent.com/pod-product-compliance
Lightning Source LLC
Chambersburg PA
CBHW030058170426
43197CB00010B/1573